Fear of Failure
Fear of Not Trying

O.Robinson

Table of Content

Dedication 3
Acknowledgement 4
Forewords 5
Recommendation 9
Chapter 1 Would've, Could've, Should've 10
Chapter 2 Hot'Lanta 13
Chapter 3 It Was All a Dream 16
Chapter 4 Impact 19
Chapter 5 Betrayal 23
Chapter 6 My Time 26
Chapter 7 Africa 30
Chapter 8 Biggest Fear 34
Chapter 9 Artists Rock the Mic 39
Chapter 10 The Juggling Act 42
Chapter 11 I Cheated So What 46
Chapter 12 Mastering Your Mind 51
Chapter 13 Get Out of Your Own Way 54
Chapter 14 Time Has No Age 57
Chapter 15 Practical Steps 62
Afterword 65
Personal Notes 66
Quotes I Live By 68
Love Versus Fear 70
Poem by Mimosa Queen of life 70
Call of Action 72
About the Author 73
Book Me 76

Dedication

This book is dedicated to the Underdogs. To anyone who feels like their situation is holding them back from greatness or has been too scared to take that leap of faith for whatever reason. I dedicate this book to all my strong Kings and Queens out there; let your voice be heard. Go for your dreams, and don't let anyone else define who you are.

This book is in two parts, the first part talks about my story, followed by the lessons I've learned, and how I overcame the fear of failure. Now, I realize everybody's story and journey is different, and some may say this is merely a music autobiography, and I would say it is to a degree. Although my path or career choice may be different from yours, you can easily insert your own career choice there. Yours may not be music, but it could be a fear of starting your own business. The actual path doesn't matter; the principals of what you can take away from this book are the same.

I struggled with this for several reasons, although I wanted to make this book strictly about how I overcame my fear of failure and how you can do the same. If you do not know my story, my struggles and setbacks then you cannot understand why I chose the steps I took and how I overcame my fear of failure. I honestly was afraid to take this leap and write my story. I was scared no one would support me, but I realize, I must not be afraid to go after any and everything I want in life. Writing a book has always been a dream of mine and now a reality. May this book encourage you to take flight!

Last, but certainly not least, it's dedicated to my grandmother Carolyn Thompson, who transitioned a few days before this release.

Acknowledgement

I would like to acknowledge some special people in my life who supported me along my journey; my two amazing boys Dekori and Christian Robinson, you push me to strive higher and never let anything hold me down. To my dad and mom, Rosaline Elliott; my rock, I learned it all from you. To my dearest Terrance Hutchinson, your words of encouragement, support, and love have meant so much to me. To my baby sisters Nekeysha & Alicia, you always lift me up, Thank You!

To my friends: ShayButta (inside joke) and Wesley Floyd, Tim Ray, Kim Goudej, Cappie, Billy Johnson, Princess Moradeun Ogunlana, Dr. William Woods, The amazing Reverend Dr. Gregory Sutton, and Ambassador Dr. Cappriccieo M. Scates. Your guidance, love and support are appreciated.

To my spiritual brothers who always have my back and are quick to pray for me and with me: Neal Vannoy, and Marc J, I appreciate you guys so much, your prayers have helped me overcome my fears. To my beastie's: Havens (Champ) Williams a.k.a my Havous, LaMonte' Swann, Ken Burwell, Peaches, and Georgie Renz. Thanks!

To my fantastic team: My designer, Vanessa Henderson (House of Van Miller), My hair stylist- Monti (The Full Monti), My glam squad Paris (Eye Candy Glam Bar & Studio), my wardrobe stylist, Johonda (Alis by Johonda), my photographer, David Price. I love all of you guys!

To everyone who has believed in me, offered a kind word of encouragement, purchased this book, donated to one of my causes, shared my picture or music video, downloaded my CD, or came out to one of my shows! From the bottom of my heart, I thank you!

Forewords

As is often said, nothing beats a failure, but a try. As Franklin D. Roosevelt stated, "the only thing we have to fear is fear itself." So, what are we really afraid of? Is it failure, trying, success, falling short of our goals, what others may think, making the wrong decisions, breaking the glass ceiling? Whatever it may be, F.E.A.R. is nothing more than False Evidence Appearing Real. In other words, we create our realities and fear is something that we have complete control over.

In her book, Oleathia 'Butta' Robinson identifies her fears, but cleverly establishes how those fears were only obstacles when she gave them power. As someone once put it, we are all in one of three phases in our lives. We are either in a storm, headed towards a storm or we have just exited a storm. If that be the case, the question becomes what will you do at each phase? Butta points out those moments and what she did during those times to overcome.

The interesting part is, she would visit my office during some of these times and I had no idea what was behind her experiences and what role I was playing within her bigger story. Yes, we all have stories to tell and we never know the depths of each person's growth. I would witness a beautiful, witty, driven and superbly talented artist entering my office each time bringing great energy, passion and grace to the atmosphere, but never truly knowing the behind the scenes of her smile. In fact, when you are in my position as a seeker of talent, you become programmed to look for, "the it factor." Butta has always exemplified the necessary tools to succeed within the music business as it relates to having what it takes, but now I know the story behind her greatness.

Finding success is often not as difficult as one believes once we overcome our fears. It is the stories of others and their triumphs over fear that gives us the courage to keep pressing ahead. This book captures a story of adversity while also sharing an honest point of view from a place of the heart; hurting more if she didn't try and now sharing her experiences to help others.

Ambassador Dr. Cappriccieo M. Scates, Ph.D.

Nothing is more crippling in life than the fear of failure. Human beings will stand strong against wildfires, floods, earthquakes, tornados, snowstorms, typhoons and sickness. In those matters, humans have proven their ability to persist and to recover after facing great loss of life and property. The fear of failure can be far more devastating in the minds of human beings than anything else. Over the last years, as a college professor I have witnessed students that were crippled by a fear of math and a fear of public speaking. They carried on an internal dialogue that kept them trapped by their thinking. When a person is convinced that they are going to fail, they often commit to failure with their thoughts and actions.

William G.Woods PhD

Ms. Oleathia Robinson stands as an example of one person that uses every ounce of energy that she has and every resource that she can find in order to legally and ethically pursue success in life. She has successfully and simultaneously worn the hats of mother, college student, entertainer, and Chapter President for the largest honor society in the world. Fear does not control her. She is driven to overcome it and other challenges that she is faced with because success is the only alternative that she will settle for.

Reverend Dr. Gregory Anthony Sutton, Senior Pastor

Recommendation

In "Fear of Failure," Oleathia "Butta" Robinson aptly portrays that self-belief is the key step to look at failure as the incredible learning experience that it often is. I highly recommend this great book.

....HRH Princess Dr. Moradeun Ogunlana, Author of "The Achiever's Power"

Chapter 1

Would've, Could've, Should've

Ever feel like you were right on the cusp of something great and then – poof! It was gone? Well, that was me. I've had so many "almost" encounters: I almost got the record deal, almost got the placement, almost got the perfect manager, almost got the tour of my dreams. Almost, would've, could've, should've…it seemed like the story of my life. I was good, but not good enough. I've always felt like I was a reject, until one day I got sick and tired of being sick and tired. I'd gotten to the point where, if I was going to succeed or fail, it was going to be on my own terms. No longer was I going to let others determine if I was good enough, thin enough, young enough or pretty enough to get in the game. It was then, crying to God one day feeling utterly hopeless, that I decided to take fate into my own hands. So, how did I get here, at this place and space in time? Well, that requires us to go back.

Even as a kid, I've always had a sense of greatness inside of me, like my life had meaning. I had a purpose, and that purpose was music. I remember it so vividly. I was four years old, and I heard and saw the most beautiful woman, dressed in a long gown singing on TV. I was mesmerized by her smile; her grace, and I wanted to be just like her. Oh, how I wished I were a member of her family. I ran upstairs, threw on my pretty dress, grabbed my boa and shades, and ran to the kitchen to get my wooden spoon (aka my microphone). I was ready to give a show!

There, I stood in my great grandmother's home, singing in front of the TV with Diana Ross and the Supremes – and at that moment, I knew exactly what I wanted to do with my life. I began as with most kids -- singing at church. Then, my cousins and I formed a singing group called N.O.L.T (None Other Like This), and we began perfecting our craft.

After school, we rehearsed. On the weekends, we rehearsed. I ate and slept music and we started entering singing contests. By the tender age of 12, I had so many forms of rejection under my belt. I was a pro at hearing the word "NO" or "you're good but, just need a little more practice," "keep trying, there's always next time." Each time we lost, I went home and analyzed our steps and our vocals, trying to figure out what I needed to do to become better. I began writing down my feelings.

These feelings started to take the form of melodies and my first song L.O.V.E was birthed. For a 13-year-old, the song was great, and it gave me the momentum I needed to keep working at it. With dedication and lots of practice, our group began to win the talent shows, and bigger doors started opening up for us.

Throughout both middle school and high school, I didn't attend any parties, school games or social events and it wasn't because I wasn't allowed. I had a hunger for music. Instead, I was at home in the mirror singing, exercising and conditioning myself for what was to come.

This was by choice. As time progressed, the faces of my group had many makeovers. But what remained the same was me and my hunger and burning desire to hear myself on the radio, to see myself on TV, to win and perform at the Grammys – to be a superstar!

No one – and I mean no one – could have told me differently. Little did I know, I was preparing myself for what was to come. All through high school, it was like I had a visor on: I ate, slept and breathed music. And if you weren't talking music, well, we simply had nothing to talk about. Even then, I had that burning desire and that sense of knowing music was my calling and something I would be doing for the rest of my life.

Chapter 2

Hot'Lanta

At age 15, in the 11th grade in 1994, my group N.O.L.T was traveling back and forth to Atlanta working with AJ Alexander who was apart of Usher's camp. It felt like I was in boot camp with my mom (aka momager) and our co-manager, AJ Alexander. They had us running up and down steps, singing, doing pushups – you name it! My mind and body had to be conditioned. I could have sworn we were kin to Joe Jackson 'cause my momma, Rosaline, nor AJ played. They demanded greatness and I demanded it of myself. I didn't have a typical upbringing. I faced choices like going to prom or going to Miami for Queen Latifah and performing at 'How Can I be Down.' Music was my life, my drug of choice, and to me, the only option. Nothing else mattered. We were traveling so much back and forth to Atlanta working in the studio, that my mom packed up and moved me, my sister and my group there. I had arrived or so I thought. I stayed in Executive Village, which was almost equivalent in my eyes to Motown back in those days. Back then, A Few Good Men lived there, as well and other artists. Through my attorneys, Moore and Hawthorne, we were practically a part of LA Face Records. We attended pool parties and other events with Goodie Mob, TLC, Usher, A Few Good Men, Lil Zane, Outkast, and so many more.

Everyone was young, fresh and new on the scene. Some of the artists had just released their singles, and some were still in the studio.

Back then, Usher lived in a townhome. I got my very first speeding ticket while picking him up to take him back to my house. AJ, my co-manager, lived above us and I was extremely close to his sons, Hakeem (Bobby Brown's nephew) and Usher. We were a close-knit family; we worked together and played together.

Executive Village was the hot spot! All the greats stayed there. Eventually, they used part of the housing for dorms for The Art Institute. Can you imagine walking outside to see people making music, hearing drummers and keyboardist practicing and other vocalist sitting in the hallways preparing songs for their class assignments? A lot of great hits were formed there. It was heaven! So many major people came out of Executive Village; it was there that I met my idol. It's funny how people can come into your life (even for a second) and make such an impact.

I remember so vividly this beautiful, hip female bass player that started pouring words of encouragement into my life. Debra Killings was a rock star in my eyes. You didn't see (especially in those days) too many female bass players – plus, she could sing, and she was a freakin' star! Even then, I was being surrounded by the greats. I was vocal-coached by James Slaughter, and mentored by William Burke.

Atlanta was nothing like Tampa; it was fast-paced, big city lights, late nights and there were always an event or showcase taking place. We began to make a name for ourselves and peeped interest from some labels and Grammy production teams. At one point we had an opportunity to work with Silent Partner; it was between two girls groups: The Dolls and my group N.O.L.T. They ended up choosing to work with The Dolls, who eventually changed their names to Destiny's Child (I can not begin to express how this almost situation could have completely changed the course of my entire life).

Let's face it; it's never easy keeping a group together; we've all heard the stories. You have different personalities, egos; you name it, add to this; people in our ears filling our young minds with lies to pull us apart. They began saying things like "You should be the lead singer, etc. Our group started having face changes, and eventually, some of us went solo. Going solo was never a thought for me, yet giving up music was never an option.

Chapter 3

It Was All a Dream

I started doing studio work at Dallas Austin's studio, Darp, with the help of Danny Zook and Kim Smith and some amazing producers: Ricco Lumpkins, and Jasper. For a brief moment, Debra Killings' mom, Carol began managing me as well, and let me tell you something, she didn't play! Every single time I went into the studio, she would make sure that my paperwork was done correctly and that I was getting paid. I did some of the demo vocals for TLC, but Debra Killings did the actual albums. They started calling me baby Killings, which was a major compliment to me! I was just happy to be in the number, amongst all the greats. There were so many artists there who were being groomed for greatness. Artist like the beautiful and multi-talented Monica and Algebra – everybody that walked through Darp studios was a star or became a star!

My first official placement was Lil Zane's None Tonight single on January 1st, 2000 and hype was not even the word for what I was experiencing. I could hardly believe it – me, a 19-year-old teen, getting $1000 to $1500 to lay down vocals for national recording artists was so dope! I had arrived, LOL! One day while in the studio, I overheard someone talking about people needing to stay in their lanes. For example, if they played the guitar, they needed to focus on that. Or if they sung backgrounds, then they needed to focus on that and not try to produce or come out as a solo artist.

It was, right then and there, that I knew, if I stayed in that space, I would only be recognized in the industry as the background studio singer. I needed and wanted to be, so much more than just in the background (not that anything's wrong with that, but I personally wanted more). I would still come to the studio from time to time to do backgrounds, but not as much as I did before.

I began focusing on coming out as a solo artist. I went into the studio and produced a demo project, in which my new attorney shopped. I remember so vividly the day my attorney's office called to inform me that I had two record deal offers on the table: one with Warner Brothers and one with Sony Records. Both are major labels, ya' girl had made it, baby! All of my hard work: the late nights, sacrifices, sweat and tears were finally about to pay off. I could see it so clear: hearing my songs on the radio, charting on Billboard as #1 on the R&B charts, being interviewed on BET by Free and AJ, giving my award speech in which I, of course, thanked God and my mother at the Grammy's for best new artist, video of the year, and artist of the year.

Both Warner Brothers and Sony were offering me big advancements, and baby, that money was practically spent in my head – LOL. I was going to buy my mom her dream home, buy myself a townhome and get the latest Mercedes or BMW – straight top of the line (you already know I had to have the finer things in life). Shopping sprees, you name it – it was mine!

I was ready for it all. My music career would lead to me doing features with other major artists, as well as help me segue into doing guest appearances on TV/Film. And Lawd, oh Lawd, I couldn't wait for the tours! I had dreamed about being a headliner, or even opening up for a megastar on a world tour since I was 10 and this right here, was my time!

My attorney at the time was the late great Vernon Slaughter of Katz, Smith, and Cohen; his firm was one of the biggest entertainment law firms around, and they represented a lot of major artist including Mary J Blige, James Brown, Jimmy Buffett, Michael Jackson and TLC to name a few.

The day before I was to meet with him to go over our offers from both labels, an accident on the highway with me, my cousin and her friend ended all of my dreams.

Chapter 4

Impact

There I was sitting in the back seat of my cousin's car then wham, instantly, my life changed. We were hit from the back, our car spun around several times before it hit the median. My cousins' head was stuck in the steering wheel, and the emergency crew had to use the jaw's of life to break the steering wheel. The passenger's seatbelt had ripped into her friend's neck, causing her to have to go into surgery immediately. My encounter with my cousin's friend was brief as I had just met her that day, I remember she had long beautiful hair, however, the next time I saw her after the surgery, her head was shaved, and she had to wear a halo and pins to hold her head up.

As for me, the sudden impact caused my face to hit the back of the passenger's seat. I jumped out of the car and noticed oil was dripping; people ran over to help me, but I begged them to help get my cousin and her friend out the car. I was scared, a lady grabbed my hand and began praying for us, while paramedics, police and the fire department freed the ladies from the vehicle.

I had two big knots on my face, but by the time we reached the hospital, my face was completely swollen. The bone underneath my eye had been shattered, and I had blurred vision. I was in pain and scared out of my mind. There I was, having a needle injected into my arm by the anesthesiologist. She calmly tried to explain to me that the medicine she was injecting into my arm would put me in a deep sleep. Terrified does not describe my thoughts – what if I didn't wake up?

The anesthesiologist had me count down from ten to one, but before I got to eight, I was knocked out. The doctor ended up having to do surgery through my mouth, gave me stitches at the top of my gums and placed titanium plates in my face right underneath my right eye. The titanium plates were screwed into my muscles, my face was completely swollen, and I looked hideous. They told my mom the surgery should take up to three hours, but there were so many bones shattered, it ended up being a little over six hours.

My accident left me with permanent titanium plates in my face, stitches in my gums that thankfully dissolved, and drinking from a straw for six months. Drinking from a straw was extremely hard; I was so tired of drinking tomato soup and cream of broccoli. Yet, I was extremely grateful when I advanced to buttered grits and then pureed food like beef and vegetables. Man, it was like Thanksgiving Day! Finally, some variety to choose from to eat! My Godmother Denise was a big help during this rough patch of my life and helped nurse me back to health. Eventually, my stitches dissolved in my mouth but unfortunately, all of my hopes and dreams faded away too.

It was Akon who frequently visited my family and me, who encouraged me to get back out there on the music scene. But, how could I? It was almost a year later, I hadn't sung in months, and honestly, I was scared too. I didn't know if I could sing anymore, nor how I would feel. I mean…what if I tried to sing and nothing came out? Or, what if people could see the mark underneath my eye? I was broken mentally and spiritually.

The impact of getting hit in that car had completely changed the course of my life. I went back to my attorney's office a year later, and both deals were off the table. One label had revamped their music division entirely and didn't have the same A&R team, and the other label had just signed a young lady who was two or three years younger than me. I went to the third label, which had been interested in me, only to hear some tough love. The rep at this label stated, "My time had passed." You see, the new wave of signing young artist; artist like

Brittany Spears who released the single "Baby One More Time" at age 11 was in and at the old age of 19, I was practically ancient, so I was out.

Before my accident, I was in the studio with Akon on a regular basis. Back then, he was the dopest MC I had ever heard, plus he could sing. But more importantly, he was my friend. Our families were close as well. His mom, Kine, was my new adopted mom and my kids would call his mom, Grandma. I know his entire family very well.

The song "Locked Up" was an instant hit for Akon, and he became swamped going on tour, promoting his new single. Eventually, he started Konvict Music. He began signing artists like T-Pain and Lady Gaga to his label, Kon Live. It was then that I began to feel as if I was now being treated like a groupie trying to get on or something. But I was the same chick that did the hooks at the studio in Smyrna, GA and in the apartment we recorded out of before my accident. Kon would tell me that this industry was hard and destroys families, and he didn't want that for me. He told me to "be patient, little sis. Your time is coming," but when? At this time, a lot of my friend's careers had advanced to either being mega artist themselves, or they were now working with megastars. As for me, I felt like I hit a brick wall and was a complete failure.

Now, let me go ahead and put this disclaimer out there. I am not attacking anyone, I have nothing but love and respect for my friends, and I'm very proud of their accomplishments, I am merely speaking how I felt about the incidents that happened in my life. Not that anyone owed me anything but none of my friends offered to extend a hand to pull me up with them after my accident. Some of their numbers had changed, I use to be able to pick up the phone and speak directly to my friends; they would call me regularly and vice versa. But now, I had to go through their assistants to speak to them.

To be honest, I thought I would be treated the same way like before the accident or that they would extend an offer to put me on a track or have me write on a project, sing backgrounds, something, anything! I would have done that without hesitation for any of them.

Now, I truly understand that as an artist, you are busy trying to make a name for yourself and that your circle will change a little. I just didn't think it would be me looking from the outside of the circle on the sidelines, when I use to be right beside them at the table. To this day, none of them know how hurt I was, the pain of rejection is a hard pill to swallow, and it truly messes with your mind. These thoughts started to tear into my spirit, and my self-esteem was gone. With the record deals now gone and still trying to pick up the pieces after my car accident, I had a lot of psychological things I was now dealing with in my own mind, and it made me question myself – What was wrong with me? Was I not good enough, anymore? Was I really as they said too old and washed up at nineteen?

It's tough for females in a male dominated industry; especially the music industry, it always has been. Most times we are placed in two categories: either we are looked at as being easy or being a B, for standing up for ourselves. So, to make matters worse, I had music directors who promised to put me on major tours and mega-producers who wanted to work on my upcoming album that took their offers away once they found out, I wasn't open to sleeping my way to the top. I felt trapped, and I wanted out.

I fell into a deep depression. Without music, who was I? I was nothing. I accepted in my mind that I was in love with something that was not in love with me anymore. Music, my first love, took away my soul and I had nothing left. I began to fade to the black, got a 9 to 5 job, went to college, got a degree in computer programming, got married and had kids. I was living the American dream as they say. But, how many of you guys know when something is in you, you can't ignore it?

Chapter 5

Betrayal

For several years, I suppressed it, but from time to time, I would do a show here and there. I was completely miserable. So many times, I got knocked down, but I had to figure out a way to get back up. I needed to get back to my first love; I needed to get back to the music. I called up my friends at Darp studio, Kim Smith and Danny Zook, and told them I wanted back in. They placed me with this dope producer out of Belgium named Lunaman. Lunaman was the absolute truth. He had so many amazing tracks that I ended up having to call for reinforcements to help me write to them. I called on my writing partners, Homer McEwen, Jason Little, Kareem and Neph 150, and formed a writing company called Ameba Writers. I began practically living in the studio. I would go to work, check on my sons and husband, and head to the studio.

I wouldn't even see the light of day until the next morning, completely unaware of time. I would literally wash up in the bathroom at the studio after being there for six to seven hours, go back to work and then do it all over again. This was my daily routine. This was my life and a happy time and space for me. Thank God for a wonderful support system. My family, especially my husband, truly had my back. We banged out hit after hit, and I was back in my element.

Luna stayed with my family for several months. We were banging out one to two tracks a day – straight hits – and I was on a freaking roll! Luna installed Logic on my computer and set up my in-home studio. I was officially in business and could start recording inside my home. At that time, I had my writing and publishing deal with BMI. One thing my mother instilled in me at an early age was to always handle your business first. So, every single time Ameba writers worked on a song with Luna, we did the proper split sheets with all the pertinent information, i.e., writer's affiliations, split sheet %, full legal name(s), etc. Lunaman eventually went back to Belgium. By that time, we had banged out at least 20+ songs.

While back in Belgium, we received the news any writer wants to hear. Several of my songs were placed on an Artist! Sandrine was an artist from Belgium who came in second place in Euro Song. Three of my songs were placed on one of her CD's, and I had my first official single "Run Away" on her third album, I couldn't be more ecstatic! This chick was singing at award shows, TV shows, performing at major festivals in front of 30k+ people, singing my song so hype, was an understatement! The hype-ness quickly faded when I was told that Lunaman spent all of the advancement money that was given to him for our placements. How in the world could this be?

We had all of our paperwork in order, had a clear understanding of how we would split any money made on songs advancements, and we all had a copy of all of the paperwork. Luna kept all the funds and left us with the explanation that he needed the money and spent it. Livid is an understatement for how I felt. Sadly, all he put on the CD credits was my stage name, Butta. Even though he knew my legal name, he knew my BMI number associated as a writer and had a copy of the split sheets for each song, the credits read as if I didn't exist. Needless to say, it was hard trying to collect funds off her performances. I was devastated and began to close off. I found out other songs of mine were placed by him on other artists overseas and here I was penniless and didn't even have the writers credit to show for any of my work.

Feeling utterly betrayed, I didn't want to write any more songs for anyone else. I was closed off to doing collaborations with producers, and I didn't care to write for other artists what so ever. I was done. I felt as if I had missed the mark on so many occasions. These almost, would've, could've, should've, moments were played out. Now, I'm not at all a violent person, but the Taurus bull in me would have come out at that moment, the way I felt. It's a good thing that he was overseas, and I didn't have access to him.

Here I was again, at this place and space in time. I wanted to hide from all the pain, rejection and betrayal that I continued to feel from my first love. I felt as if I had missed the mark on so many occasions, and music was now my curse, a cruel punishment that God bestowed upon me. So close, yet so far away. Music was my fairy nightmare.

Chapter 6

My Time

I swear, there is something about music that draws me back in each time. It's almost as if it has a magnetic hold on me. One day, I ran into my old co-manager, AJ, who suggested I form my own band and do my own thing. There was just one problem now: my 9 to 5 consumed all of my time. You see, I was so busy building someone else's dream for their company that I didn't have any time to spare for myself. So, with heavy hesitation, I left my corporate job in 2007 and all of the securities it had to offer.

My job was like my security blanket; I knew that every two weeks, I could count on it to be there. I wasn't happy there—not at all—but hey, it was a job. Stepping out on faith was a hard thing for me to do. I no longer had my benefits or my 401k. I was terrified, to say the least. My household was accustomed to a particular lifestyle by this time. My husband had recently left his job to pursue his own entrepreneurship, so it was scary times in my household, a whole lot of unknowns. I did not know what was going to happen from day to day or how we were going to make ends meet with neither one of us having steady income coming into the household now.

We ran through our savings. But, this had to be one of the most liberating times of my life. We were broke and barely hanging on at certain times, but we were happy. Our bond was stronger toward one another. We had a roof over our heads. Our kids were healthy and safe, and their needs were being met. But most importantly, we were free in the pursuit of happiness.

I had to bet on me, even if no one else would. What I learned was that you can't let someone else's opinion about you determine who you are. If I was going to fail, it was going to be on my own terms. So, I at least, had to give it a try. What did I have to lose? There is nothing like doing something you genuinely have a passion for. It wasn't about the money for me. I would have given my last dime, I sat my broke tail in my home and banged out the best songs that represented me and everything I wanted to say. I worked with some of the dopest producers in Atlanta and produced my very own album that I released on my own label "Switch Lanes." I was so proud of myself. I also signed a publishing deal with Royalty Network out of New York, and got out of my contract with BMI and moved over to Sesac.

Back then, Sesac was truly happening. Our division was run by the one and only Cappriccieo Scates. What I loved most about Sesac was that you couldn't just pay your way to get in and be an affiliated writer with them. You had to be invited in. Everyone was treated the same, no matter their level. He believed anyone could have that next big hit and treated everyone with dignity and respect.

Back then, everyone wanted to call Sesac home. Before the ink was even dry on my deal, Cappriccieo had worked out a meeting with Trevor Gale, the Vice President of Writer Publisher Relations for SESAC in NY and when I flew to LA, I met and hung out with VP James Leach. All three were/are amazing men. Performing at the Sesac Christmas event opened many doors for me. It was the perfect platform to introduce myself as an artist and showcase my band. I was so honored when Sesac added me to their magazine's Up and Coming New Artist section. That was a tremendous platform to be featured on. Two months later, I had my album and music video release party for my debut album, Switch Lanes.

The venue was completely packed. In fact, I'm told there was a line leading down the street of people trying to get into my event. I had teenagers, Chloe and Halle, open up my show (It's no surprise they are now signed to Beyoncé; these girls are fantastic and had a work ethic even at a young age that was untouchable). My release party was a major success, and I introduced to the world: my band, background singers, my dancers, my CD, and music video. I had such an outpouring of love and support from people who helped make this moment so special for me. I want to take this time to say thank you for everyone who was involved in my CD, my performance, my release party, my music video or anything that was behind the scenes. It was truly a group effort.

It looked like Lady Luck had finally shined her light on me! Once you put yourself out there and have intent, the universe delivers. I was blessed to get hired by the beautiful and multi-talented Kim Burse for BET's Hip Hop Award Show performance with NAS. I performed as a background vocalist with Grammy country artist, Zac Brown, and provided background vocals for the album of the one and only legendary award-winning rock group, Collective Soul. I even got a phone call to work with Janet Jackson, thanks to Billy at Crossover studio. Meeting her was a dream come true, her demeanor, and her poise was all that. She was freaking beautiful and very soft-spoken. I was just happy to be in the room.

It wasn't anything major, and no, I didn't have the privilege of going on tour or anything like that with her. But that didn't matter to me. I worked with Ms. Jackson (if you're nasty)! I also worked on Chilli of TLC's solo project and was brought in for a soundtrack, doing background vocals for the girl R&B group, Blaque. Also, thanks to my mentor, William Burke, I did a studio session for The Dream for his upcoming tour. I was back baby!

It was during my Sesac performance; I met a good friend who worked for V103. He connected me with one of the promoters who booked bands at Centennial Park. My initial date scheduled to perform there got rained out, but another artist, Seven, was gracious enough to let me open his show. There I stood, my third official show with my band in front of 3000 plus people, it was like a dream come true for me! My crew held me down, and we had a killer show.

Chapter 7

Africa

Centennial Park performance was a success, and ten minutes after I got off stage, I met with CC, an incredible vocalist whom I had spoken to over the phone. He was putting a band together to tour in Addis Ababa, Africa. He had come to check me out and officially made the offer. Through the years, I had been approached by several people to go overseas to tour in Japan, Canada, and Dubai, but either the contract was too long, they weren't talking enough money, or something just didn't seem right with the offer. But this offer was perfect: all expenses paid, performing only four nights, doing two 45-minute sets a week, plus it was only a three-month contract, as opposed to the 12 to 24-month contracts I had been offered prior. Also, we had two drivers. They gave each of us our own cell phones and our own rooms, plus, they brought over one of our family members with all their expenses paid for two weeks. I was able to negotiate doing some of my own material at the shows. So, this was a win-win situation for me.

Africa was amazing. My eyes had never seen all the wonders that I saw there! Mother Earth was so rich and beautiful. Words truly can't express how incredible this place was, but it also was a cultural shock. I had never seen goats, chicken and bulls walking in the middle of the street. Markets with skinned meat for sale on the side of the road like we see during the Sweet Auburn festival that showcases vendors. These meat stores were on every corner. If you wanted some, you would point to the parts you wanted. They would wrap it up with white paper, and you would take it home to eat. Most ate it raw, adding nothing more than the spices that it was dipped in. That was different for me to see.

We stayed at the Sheraton, which was like a mega castle to me. Inside those walls was paradise. They had several restaurants offering different types of food. I ate and tried things I hadn't dreamed of trying before, like lamb. Their meat was fresh and free from preservatives. I saw and tasted the difference between real sugars versus the processed sugar we have here in America. I tasted the local food like injera and fir fir. Both were different but good. During a wedding ceremony, I was served himbasha, which is like celebration bread used at special occasions.

I saw poverty and wealth; I also saw riches everywhere – beautiful homes, amazing landscapes, and different languages. I witnessed people living in mansions like homes, while the next set of houses were mud homes and tin homes using the daylight as their form of light. Some used large tin pans as if it was a tub for their bathing and cooking chamber. I had only seen things like that on TV, so these were cultural shocks for me. I witnessed people using rocks as their pillows sleeping outside. I had personally never seen grandmothers looking like they had to be in their late 70's walking up and down the mountains daily with eucalyptus branches on their backs, or kids carrying yellow plastic containers to gather water. They used this water to cook, bathe and drink. The men were off to work while the women tended the homes.

I didn't see crime; instead, I saw peace, harmony, and oneness. I have met some of the best people in Africa that I'm proud to call my friends. These are people who I truly respect and appreciate. They showed me nothing but love and made me feel welcomed. Africa made me more humble and appreciative of my life. We take for granted the little things like water, lights, and food. I remember walking the Blue Nile, and the kids walked alongside us asking for pens. Some of these children had no shoes on, and this bothered me. I spoke to my mother about this and asked her if she could help me collect supplies. She said she could do one better, so she contacted her hospital that she worked at

'Children's Healthcare,' and they collected school supplies as well as donated medical supplies to the local African hospital.

The agency that hired me flew my mother to Africa. The next time I came back to the Blue Nile, I had supplies with me. Who would think something so simple as flip-flops or pen and pencils would be appreciated and wanted. During my mom's trip there, she volunteered at the local hospital and even helped deliver a baby. I swear, the hospital wanted to keep my mother there. She received a letter from the prime minister for her contributions while she was there.

Another thing that caught me off guard in Bahir Dar was witnessing, mothers cleaning their children out of the same lake that people were washing their clothes. They swam in and drank from the water while animals were being bathed in the same water. It made me see the harsh reality of life. They were doing what they had to do to survive and using what they had around them to do it. We sometimes take things like drinking water and separate water for washing for granted. This experience made me appreciate what I had. No longer did I complain about little things. While my mom was there, the prime minister died, and we attended the viewing.

There were thousands of people there of different tribes and languages, all paying tribute and homage to this great man. I saw unity during the home-going ceremony. Although we didn't speak the same language, we respected one another. I cried like a baby. You would have thought I knew him personally, but I felt the pain and the love they felt for this man. When an official passes, government shuts down for several days to mourn. Therefore, all shows were canceled.

On a more cheerful note, I sang and hung out with a prince, ambassadors and city council members. We were flown to other parts of Africa on the weekends, and all my expenses were paid while we stayed at various resorts. There were people screaming my name and fainting at the shows. People said they would never wash their faces or hands again because I touched them. It was totally insane in a great way! Afro 105.3 started letting me sit in on one of their shows as a guest, and they put my single, Strange Love, in rotation on their station.

I truly appreciated the experience and hope to return one day on another tour in Addis Ababa with my boys.

Chapter 8

Biggest Fear

I've always been a family woman. My core values are God, family, and music. My husband and boys mean the world to me. We were a very close-knit family, and they were supportive of my career. One of my biggest fears about going overseas was that my boys would forget about me and that I would become distant with my husband. My husband encouraged me to go to Africa. He mentioned to me how performing has always been my dream to tour. Every time I got an offer for an opportunity, I would come up with excuses as to why I should not take the gigs. I would say things like, "I would be gone too long", "and my boys are too young." I couldn't help but hear in the back of my head Akon's words – that touring and getting out there as an artist destroys relationships. I didn't want any parts of that. But when the offer for Africa came with all the extra perks – including my husband being able to come to Africa to visit – I accepted.

My husband flew over, and I was so excited to share this experience with him. I had been away in other states and had late nights in the studio, but never had I been gone for this long away from my boys and my man. It was there during my first tour that I began to see we weren't in the same space anymore. For the first time, when my husband came over to Africa, jealousy began to show its ugly head. Unnecessary arguments started to take place. He didn't like me smiling and talking to all of these gentlemen. But, on and off stage in public, you are technically still on stage and must act accordingly. All eyes are on you. So, people would come up to me after I finished my show to speak and take pictures. This was all a part of the game of showbiz.

I remember so vividly. It was New Year's Eve, and we had just gotten off stage. Champagne was pouring, and everybody who was somebody was at the Sheraton for the New Year's Eve after party. Ambassadors and political figures offered me drinks left and right and were striking up conversations with me. They took offense if you didn't drink with them or make the time to engage in what they were saying. It was there that jealousy began to show its dark side. Unfortunately, an argument broke out between us. My husband turned to me and calmly but intensely stated that "If I smiled in another man's face, we were going to have problems."

I was in complete shock. He had never spoken to me that way. I wasn't disrespecting him. He was right there, being introduced to every person that came up to me. For the first time, I realized that it might have been a mistake coming to Africa. I realized that this was hard for both of us and neither one of us had dealt with this type of situation of being separated for this long. He left Africa with us being on shaky terms.

Although we discussed and worked it out, you could tell it lingered on in the back of our minds. My focus was to get to Africa, make the right connections to advance my career, collect my coins and provide a better life for my family. I had never cheated on my husband. I would be lying if I said I didn't have offers – of course, I had offers. But, I had the same type of proposals in the states plenty of times. I didn't accept the offers then, and I certainly was not going to do that over in Africa. It did make me reflect and wonder what he was doing now at home. Usually, the one that's accusing you of doing things is the very one who's typically doing something, and it's out of guilt or fear that makes them react and now place blame and fault on you.

You see, I had already dealt with adultery with my husband when my second son was born. He wasn't even a few months old, and then again, a few years later with a different woman. Now, you may wonder why I didn't leave the first time. Well, that's simple. I loved my husband, and raising two kids on my own was not an option. Besides, I was not going to give another woman my man. I had several years vested into us, and I didn't want my husband to stray again.

Unfortunately, I started seeing signs of this when I returned from my first tour. He started sleeping in the other room, claiming he didn't want to wake me. We hadn't touched one another for months. The tension in the house was thick. Six months later, I went back to Africa for a second time. By this time, our communication with one another was at a very slim minimum. It had felt as if we were merely roommates, only sharing space to raise our kids. Our longest conversation was when he was dropping me off at the airport. So, I went back to Africa, feeling an empty void. I was barely able to reach him on the phone. He started taking extra trips to Tampa, but this time, staying at hotels as opposed to with his family members like we did when it was our boys, his daughter, and I. He stopped putting money into our family account, even though he was still working. My second trip to Africa was horrible.

When your house isn't in order, nothing is right. My mind was all over the place. It wasn't the same crew as before: different females in the band led to different attitudes amongst us all. I was already dealing with madness at home, so I couldn't entertain too much more. I began to close myself off from the world, only hanging out with one guy. Our bond with one another grew stronger during that time; he became the shoulder I cried on.

I came back home confused and angry. My account was empty; the house was a wreck and marriage was damn near over. It hadn't gotten better. One day, while looking for an item of mine in my husband's toiletry bag, I saw something that a married man shouldn't have, that gave me a clear indication another female was in his life again. Needless to say, enough was enough. Without going heavy into details for the sake of my children, my marriage was officially over after 13 years. My divorce took several years, my husband had already moved out of the house and moved on with his life with another.

It was during this time that my bond with another guy grew into so much more. My husband and I were separated, and he had already moved on with another. He was displaying his new girl all on Facebook to the world before our divorce was even finalized. I honestly thought this new guy could be the one. Looking back, I realize he was just someone to help me get through my rough times. I foolishly thought it was love. But in the end, I was played for two of the years that we were together and he ended up marrying the very woman he swore to me was merely an old groupie friend who he went to school with years ago. So, there I was, heartbroken twice. I had no song to sing; my heart was heavy. Here I was divorced, alone, depressed and raising my boys on my own.

One day, I was so stressed out; I passed out while at Apache Café, a local music spot in Atlanta. I don't remember blanking out or hitting the back of my head. All I know is that when I opened my eyes, I could see my friend moving her mouth, but couldn't hear a word she was saying. Eventually, I began hearing her voice, and she helped me up. They helped me get outside to get some fresh air. I sat down, and slowly drank some water and regained all of my senses. My mom insisted that I go to the doctor to get a cat scan. So, the next day, I went. The doctor put me on depression and anxiety pills and referred me to a therapist. I hated talking to a therapist; to me talking about my divorce made it worse. I didn't get married with plans of getting a divorce. I didn't like talking about my feelings, or all of the things I'd failed at. These sessions in my mind, were reminders of my failures.

Suicidal thoughts filled my mind, and my life was a complete mess. I had fallen so hard. All I saw was darkness, and I just wanted it to end. The meds made me feel like a zombie. I couldn't eat, couldn't sleep. I could barely get out of bed. I cried so much until the tears just stopped flowing. Suicidal thoughts were getting stronger in my head, and I honestly started to believe the world would be better off if I weren't in it.

I found myself on the side of the expressway contemplating if I should end it all, I had convinced myself that nobody would even care or notice that I was gone. But, then I thought about my boys, what mental impact that would have on them, had it not been for my children, I promise you, I would have checked out.

Chapter 9

Artists Rock the Mic

It was through my tears and disappointments that I found joy in serving others. I began feeding the homeless, and in doing so, I realized how blessed I was. I thought about how much worse it could be, how I shouldn't complain and how, instead, I should be thanking God for everything. For a year or two, I contemplated how I could help, but what I could do? Then it hit me – I wanted to use my talents to bless others, but how? I created a plan and while at my birthday dinner, I presented a website presentation to my friends.

I told them my idea for my nonprofit organization that I wanted to start. All the kinks weren't worked out yet, but I knew what I wanted. I've always been one who can conceive an idea or desire in my mind and immediately devise a plan to get there. For months, I sat with my closest friends coming up with ideas on how to make an impact. But, I needed to hone in on a specific cause.

It was suggested that we focus on homeless college students, and Kennesaw State became the primary focus for our organization. That's how my non-profit foundation, Artists Rock The MIC (Motivating Individuals in the Community), was formed. We began devising a plan to do a "We Are the World"-type concert, bringing in all genres together under one roof. We went to business meetings to network and obtain sponsorships to help us with our concert. While talking about my organization, a gentleman approached me and told me he used to be that homeless college student that ironically use to attend Kennesaw State. He proceeded to tell me that he went from dorm to dorm. He slept on various friends' couches known as couch hopping and slept in his car.

He used the gym's locker room to take showers and ate out the cafeteria's trashcans for food. He said it got so bad that the cafeteria locked the trash doors and left a bag with food and a note saying, "Please stop eating out of here; you can get sick." I asked him if he would be my keynote speaker at my concert. It's one thing to have someone tell you about homeless college students, but to hear him and see him first hand was much more impactful. During our concert that he spoke at, we presented a check to Kennesaw State to be donated toward their homeless division. The event was a major success!

Kat's Cafe is a very known spot in the heart of downtown, and the owner, Kat, agreed to let me host monthly events to give back. The outpouring from both the music community and supporters was overwhelming. I've had both major and independent artist grace the stage. Artists like; National Recording Artist, Tony Terry, Jazze Pha, Ken Ford, Making of the Band Brain H. From The Voice Beth Spangler & Franc West, Ryan Kilgore, gospel recording artist Damita Haddon Chandler, Ricco Barrino. From America's Got Talent Xavier Lewis, Brandon Blue, Vawn Simms, Mia and SO many super talented men and women. There have been too many to name that have blessed the stage, each one talented and each one I'm grateful for. Month after month, we were able to bless the community: we collected 2000 water bottles for Flint Michigan, sent shoes to Haiti, purchased gas cards and donated them to I Will Survive, Inc. to get chemo patients back and forth from chemo.

We collected toiletry items for Homeless Vets and presented this to I Honor Your Service to America. Hosted coat drives, school supply drives, canned good drives, blanket drives – you name it, we have done it all. We performed for the Fulton County Sheriff's department but our primary goal is bringing awareness and funding to homeless college students working with Kennesaw State to make a change.

Had it not been for some fantastic people in my life who

believed in me and became the backbone of my organization, my organization wouldn't be possible. I want to take this time to personally say thank you to everyone who believed in my vision and helped in any way. I truly appreciate each one of you. Especially my core ARM team – a special thank you to Karen and Jae Qwon, who were my backbones in my beginning stages. Thank you to my advisory board: Ken Burwell, Tami Hill, Reverend Sutton of Jackson Memorial Baptist Church, Sheriff Ted Jackson of Fulton County, CatDogg of Steve Harvey's Morning show, and Paris Murphy Dr. Your advice helps me to stay on the right path. For three in half years we consistently threw concerts monthly. However, trying to juggle being in school, raising my boys, touring and life in general has made me now turn to hosting quarterly events to raise money for and bring awareness to our cause. There are currently over 1100 students at Kennesaw State that are homeless. Can you imagine trying to maintain your grades while worrying about your next meal or where you will rest your head that night? I am currently in college and can't fathom how I could successfully succeed in school if I were in that situation.

One thing I know is that music is universal. We are bringing people together for a great cause. If I can help one student or one person in general, then I'm happy. But I truly believe there is strength in numbers – the more people that get involved, the better.

If you would like to partner with my team or get more information on how you can become involved, all of my contact information is available at the back of this book, and you can visit

Artistsrockthemic.com website.

Chapter 10

The Juggling Act

For years, I have been blessed with performing on many stages statewide and abroad. I go overseas as a guest entertainer performing for cruise lines in the main theater, giving a one-night-only show. I've had the pleasure of opening for the Kentucky Derby for three years in a row and at the Duke Presidential ball. I've even performed at one of the Presidential Inaugurations. I've sung for: Dr. Bernice King, judges, ambassadors and other political officers, and as well as for the Prime Minister of Bahamas. My most significant achievement was performing in the Dominican Republic as the headliner for New Year's Eve, in front of 9,000 people.

I brought with me, my 10-piece band, plus my assistant. You would have thought I was Beyoncé or Rihanna! This place had our picture on the billboards throughout the resort. They had three LED screens above the stage and drones flying over us, capturing and displaying the performance on the screens. Fire and lasers were coming from the stage as if they were programmed to come on and off with certain words that I sung. It was magical, and nothing has topped that moment! A dream of mine is to tour with my boys, so as you can imagine, it was truly a blessing to be able to take my boys with me to the Bahamas for one of my shows. Unfortunately, I ended up injuring myself on the second day we were there and twisted my knee.

We stayed in the Bahamas for almost a whole week, and I was in horrible pain. I had to make my show an intimate setting, sitting on a stool to sing as I could not bear standing or any sudden movements with my knee. Thankfully, my client couldn't tell how much pain I was in.

You see, we artists have to push through sore throats, feeling fatigued, having the flu – you name it. I knew I had to push through. The same night I returned home from the Bahamas, I immediately went to the ER.

They informed me that my knee was severely fractured and that I shouldn't wear heels or do any type of dancing for at least six months. They gave me crutches and a soft cast that I could take on and off and told me to stay off my feet. I remember this day clearly – it was a Saturday night, around midnight to be exact. But, by that Tuesday, I was headed to Spain for a week, followed by Aruba and then Jamaica for my shows.

As an entrepreneur, I couldn't afford to have too many days off. You see, I don't get paid time off. If I don't perform, my kids don't eat. But this injury had honestly slowed me down. I tried to put heels on only when necessary. My pain level was high, but I had to push through for the sake of providing for my family. One day, as I sat in pain, I cried out, "Lord, I'm broken, I'm injured, I have all of these desires in my heart, that aren't fulfilled and I feel like I'm a failure. Am I fooling myself chasing after my dreams? Perhaps, I'm being stubborn, and you've already shown me that it's not going to happen. Is this all there is for me, to almost get that tour or almost get that placement? Will I ever hear my songs on the radio? Will I ever experience a major tour with a major artist, like my friends? Will I ever find love? What is my purpose in life, cause I'm lost?"

God and I have our own way of communicating, I have some sincere heart to heart conversations with him. Sometimes, my talks are angry. I didn't understand how I could be so obedient and focused for these many years, yet not be where I wanted to be with my career, my finances or love life. I swear, I've quit so many times and was furious with God. My dreams and aspirations are to win several Grammys, hear my music on the radio, tour on major tours as an opening act, and headliner and travel the world with my boys and my man. I want so badly to perform on Black Girls Rock and at Essence.

It just felt like these things were just dreams that would never be accomplished and I was kidding myself. I've learned that we all are our own worse critics. Even though I haven't quite gotten all that I've conceived in my head for my life, God has blessed me with milestones along the way and lessons that I needed to learn to advance to the next level for my next chapter in life. I can't beat myself up all the time. I needed to stop and smell the roses and realize that I am doing an amazing job. I may not be where I want to be, but I'm not where I use to be, and as long as I am making progress forward, it's a step in the right direction.

While going through my divorce, I decided to return to school. I needed a distraction from all the craziness that was happening in my world. It's no secret, I've never been super fond of school, I believe you should go to school to figure out your path and what career you want out in life. However, my thoughts have always been that I'm doing exactly what I love to do and school can't teach me that. I must admit, I'm actually glad I went back. It has been extremely challenging, especially with raising my boys – adjusting to all of their schedules, touring abroad, studio sessions, rehearsals, etc. I'm obtaining a degree in Marketing and Public Relations at Ashford University.

School has pushed me to become the leader I always knew I was. I'm proud to say; I'm thriving in school, maintaining a 3.80 GPA. Ashford wrote a success story on me, and I am now forever embedded in their archives! I currently serve as the Golden Key International Honours Society President for the Ashford University Chapter as the first black president, which is an accomplishment within itself. I've worked in their mentorship program, and the school has sent me to leadership seminars in other states with all expenses paid. I graduate May 5, 2019, Magna Cum Laude, all honors with a double major, and I'm a member of Alpha Sigma Lambda. I worked hard for my A's, late nights; horrible Internet connections overseas, sweat and tears but I did it, for me! I needed to show myself that I had what it takes, and I wanted to show my boys that if I could do it, so could they.

My amazing boys, Dekori and Christian are following in my footsteps. Both have been acting and modeling since the age of 7. Dekori is SAG eligible from his national TV debut on Drop Dead Divas and Christian has been in major commercial campaigns for Belk's and others. Unfortunately, during my divorce, trying to juggle everything was too much. So they took a break on acting and stopped working with their agent. Fast forward, they are now in high school. Dekori is a running back on the football team and runs track the 100, 200, 400 and 4x1. Christian is on the drumline and also works with the AMP Music Series playing with the orchestra during the summer. They have begun modeling again and graced the cover of Cam Q Magazine. They recently received the Young B.O.S.S award.

My youngest son will soon introduce to the world his clothing apparel line FYE apparel (Find Your Element). Also, he is working on his own band and music project. They've been offered a radio show, where they will have various teen topics to discuss and have recently resigned with their acting agency ECT. So, juggling their schedule with mine has been quite hectic! Thank God for a stable support system.

My family has been a real Godsend.

Chapter 11

I Cheated So What

My knee injury was a wake-up call. You see, if I got sick, lost my voice, got injured and couldn't perform, then I couldn't provide for my family. So this incident forced me to have to figure out what other talents I had. I began to look at additional things I could possibly do. I had modeled before, and for years A&Rs that worked with major labels and producers would try to get me to write on other artists' projects. But, having been burnt so many times, I was scared of writing. Perhaps, now was the time for me to try again.

I had also acted in a few plays before, and I had always wanted to write a book and a stage play. I had to be open minded – what if my life was more than just music? I had to explore what other types of gifts I had. So, I started taking more modeling gigs and have been blessed to make the cover of two magazines while being featured in several others. I also began auditioning for various plays.

It was during this time; I met an amazing writer and director named Donald Gray. One day, we were talking about deep lyrics, and I told him that I am a deep writer. I proceeded to send him one of my songs, 'The Storm." He listened to the lyrics a few times and called me back, saying he could see my song being turned into a play. I informed him I had always wanted to write a play and book, but had no clue how to get started.

He told me he had written several plays and has been in that field for over 20 years. He offered to help me write the play, so why not? We already had a blueprint from my song. You see, The Storm was originally written from a situation one of my friends experienced. One day, my friend came to my house very upset and needed someone to talk to about her situation. She had been married to her hubby for well over 10 years.

Within those 10 years, they had plenty of trials and tribulations – one being that her husband was not a faithful man. He would come home all times of the night or not at all. No call, no show and frequented with several other women. He ended up having a child by another woman, and as hurt and angry as she was; she still stood by his side and forgave him time after time. They had three kids of their own, and this child made the fourth.

On the little girl's fourth birthday, my friend took her kids to the birthday party. As she was walking into the venue for the event, an altercation happened between her and the other woman. The other woman didn't want my friend there and told her to leave. She left and went to one of her guy friend's home to clear her mind. Well, one thing led to another, and she ended up being with this man. Feeling guilty, she went home and confessed to her husband what had happened. He was outraged. He shouted at her and called her out of her name. He told her he didn't trust her anymore and wanted nothing more to do with her. He left the house, and a few months later, she was served with divorce papers. As she told me this story, I was completely in disbelief, not saying that it was right, but he had the audacity to have a problem with her cheating when he had a baby and had been with several women.

This was an example of double standards of man versus woman, and I told her my idea to write a song about it. You see, a songwriter writes songs based on feelings, it's just another form of storytelling. I thought about my dear friend and began to write. The first lines of my song are, "I admit it; I did it, I cheated, so what?" I couldn't understand how it was okay for him, but not okay for her. So, having the blueprint already written, Donald and I began to build our different characters for the play.

I learned so much during this process, we would bounce ideas off of each other. I also threw in a little bit of what I personally experienced during my divorce and the other relationship I had too. Donald was a great teacher, full of creative ideas, it was all about connecting the dots, layers and making it flow. Once I understood the concept and how to write the format, I began writing some of the chapters as well. It took us a month to write the play and five month's later we had our debut show!

My first stage play, "I Cheated So What," was birthed. This dramatic play reflects the woman and man point of view and is filled with suspense; many twist and turn, laughter, comic relief, and a spiritual tug-of-war with the flesh and spirit. Can they weather the storm when they are both wrong? Check out the play to find out. We immediately began casting, selected a venue, got sponsors and began rehearsing for the big debut.

In my first play, we cast four major national recording artists including the one and only Mr. New Jack City himself – Mr. Christopher Williams. We also had Robert Curry of the R&B group- Day 26, gospel recording artist Damita Haddon Chandler; national recording artist Ricco Barrino and Mike Merrill from Oxygen Last Squad Standing.

The biggest thrill for me was hearing my commercial played on the radio and seeing the play come from a thought to paper, then from paper to the stage. It was indeed a dream come true and was the beginning of a new chapter for me. Donald doesn't realize how grateful and how special that moment was for me. Having someone believe in me and pour into me is something I will never forget. Visit icheatedsowhat.com for more information and upcoming dates.

Since then, I've caught the writing bug, and I wrote my first TV show! There were a lot of writing and rewrites, but I finally got the formula right! Now, I have a TV show that is being pitched for national

TV, and I have interest from two major networks. I'm beyond excited about this and can't wait until everyone sees it. I also have some other projects up my sleeve, but that's for later on. I'm not sharing this to brag or complain. I'm nowhere near where I aspire to be, but I'm hoping my story will en courage you to understand anything you want is possible if you get out of your own way. It's possible if you overcome your fear of failure.

Things I've learned through this journey called life is that we create our own realities and I can only speak my own truth. Every rejection has been protection and a lesson within itself for us to grasp and learn. I've had my fair share of darkness, self-doubt, self-destruction, failed relationships, friendships that have ended, divorce and financial woes.

I can recall a point in my life where I had money owed for shows I had done, but never got paid from them or barely having enough money to get to my gigs or to put gas in my car. Life has been hard, but I've learned it's what you make of it. For every NO I received, I was determined to figure out another way in – even if I had to build my own door and make my own situation. No one was going to put me in a box. I have too much to offer, and I can't let someone else's opinion of me determine who I am or will be.

I sit alone with my thoughts a lot, and as I meditate, I ask God to show me the light and to show me the way, to open new doors and to close old doors that no longer serve a purpose in my life. I'm now more open and receptive to life, to love, to happiness. I'm no longer in that dark space - anytime you turn the light on, darkness has to leave. Even now, I feel like the best is yet to come and I've merely scratched the surface of what's in store. I'm so much more than a singer. I've also stopped comparing myself to others. I would say, "God, so and so is doing this and that in their career and I'm only doing this. But, I realized I couldn't continue to do that. We all have our own journeys, our own stories to tell.

I was so busy chasing the big fish; I didn't stop and appreciate all the beautiful things, sites, people, and places God had for me.

Chapter 12

Mastering Your Mind

If only we could stop all the negative chatter in our brains, life would be much easier. You are either brainwashing yourself or being brainwashed. Really, let that sink in, you are either brainwashing yourself with positive or negative thoughts or being brainwashed; by the TV, by the news, by the radio, by other people and the words they are saying. For years, I believed what others said to me, that I was too old for the music industry, not small enough, not pretty enough, or because I didn't have what they considered a church voice, I wasn't a real singer. There were so many things I accepted as being true about myself based on how other people viewed me. Those people and things got into my subconscious mind, and I honestly thought I wasn't good enough, I thought I didn't belong, I thought I was a failure, and the sad part was I hadn't even tried.

Slowly, I began to understand the power of my own words and of others. For if I was going to succeed in this thing called life, I had to start from within and de-program all of the negative things I had come to believe was true. Fear had to be erased from my conscious and subconscious mind, and my old belief system had to go. What are you feeding your mind? What old programming do you need to get rid of? I began reading books to open my mind; my very first 'Ahh Moment', was when I read Catherine Ponder's 'Prosperity Secrets of the Ages' in which she states, "When you rule your mind you rule your world. When you choose your thoughts, you choose results".

I started feeding my mind and soul with positive affirmations, such as:

- I now dissolve in my own mind any idea that my God-given good, can be withheld from me

- Lord, thank you for the visions, I know my breakthrough is coming

- God is my source

- It is my divine destiny to succeed

- I know God controls all and will open doors that no man can shut

- Lord, I thank you for my dreams

- Lord, I thank you that it's on the way

- God, I know what You promised will come to pass

As I began to say affirmations and spoke with authority, doors began to open. I also changed my circle of influence. What and who are you allowing in your space? I chose to no-longer hang with the Debbie Downers (you know the ones), every single time you call or see them, they have something negative to say.

I wanted and needed to surround myself with people and things, that spoke positivity, that gave me hope and encouragement. I started hanging around people who would raise my vibrations, likeminded people that sought the light. Honestly, when I began to do that, I found that a black veil had been lifted, for darkness can't hide in light. I began to understand that thoughts are things and the pain of regret for me was far worse than the pain of failure.

I began listening daily to Joel Osteen, and to a man I look up to Mr. Les Brown. I played his speech 'It's Possible' over and over on

YouTube and would go to sleep with motivational speeches from speakers like Tony Robbins. Their message of hope were being embedded in my subconscious mind.

One of my mentors, Ambassador Capprreico Scates, said it best; "FEAR is nothing more then False Evidence Appearing Real."

I also say, "FEAR is only Inverted Faith."

Chapter 13

Get Out of Your Own Way

I use to hear the saying "You're in your own way" all the time, but I never knew what it meant until I got a little older. So often, we let fear paralyze us from not even trying. Mr. Zig Ziglar says Fear has two meanings. 'Forget Everything and Run,' or Face Everything and Rise.' Without trying you cannot learn any lessons, you will never know what works and what doesn't work. I know of two ladies Jen and Suzy, they both dreamt of becoming an actor, and both started on even playing fields as newbies to the industry.

The only problem was Jen was too afraid to actually take acting lessons for fear of others laughing at her; she didn't go to the auditions out of fear of not being selected. She didn't self-tape auditions and email them to the casting directors out of fear of them talking bad about her when they reviewed her taping. Her fear of failure literally stopped her dead in her tracks, and she never even gave herself the opportunity to see if she could land a role.

Suzy, on the other hand, was a risk taker; her attitude was the same as mine, if you are going to bet on anything why not bet on yourself! Being so new in the industry, she enrolled in beginners acting. After several months, advanced to intermediate, then a year later moved to advanced courses. Suzy started working with the local theater in Tennessee and began auditioning for roles. She told me in the beginning, she did horrible and had butterflies in her stomach, yet despite that, she would say a prayer before every audition and just go for it. Unfortunately, she didn't get the role, and casting director after casting director would tell her a strong 'NO', and that could have been the end of her story.

She could have done like so many of us do when the times get rough, with so many rejections, she could have just quit. But, that wasn't her ending, each time she auditioned, her confidence level got stronger and stronger, and she learned what to do and what not to do. She understood that in order to get good, you must first try. For every 'no', she turned that into a learning tool and would keep coming back to audition, determined to break into show business.

Suzy decided in order to really get an opportunity to break into showbiz she had to move to a state that had lots of opportunities, selling most of her things and leaving with $2000 in her pocket, she moved to LA. The cost of living in LA is a major difference from Tennessee. At first, she stayed with friends and would sleep on their couches, but that grew old quickly. She looked for a place of her own, but the prices even for a one-bedroom ran $1200 or more. Within less then a month, she was broke, without a job and had not landed one single audition in LA. She began taking odd jobs; she pawned her jewelry and other items. It got to the point where she wasn't able to afford the rooms at the extended stays, so she started sleeping in her car, taking showers at the truck stops and sometimes eating only once a day.

She would cry herself to sleep at night hungry, scared. She began second-guessing her decisions. Her friends and family advised her to give up and come back home, but she was determined to make it. She used any money she made to enroll in more acting classes.

One day, her acting coach told her he had a possible part for her in an independent film; she made the cut, and got a very small one-liner part. The one-liner gave her the boost she needed and encouraged her to push harder to perfect her craft. It took her 2 years of struggling before she actually made it to the big screen; she has now been on several TV shows and just landed a role in a featured film. Was it hard for Suzy? Yes of course, but you have to have a desire to keep going, against all the odds.

Honestly, no story is alike, but one thing is true, if you don't start, if you never give yourself the opportunity to see what you're made of, you will never know where it will lead you. The problem with so many of us, myself included is, we want things easy, and we get discouraged when it doesn't happen in the timeframe we've envisioned it should take in our own minds. If it's something that's in your heart, go for it. Have enough faith in yourself and your creator to understand he won't give you those desires or visions if they weren't possible. Get out your own way and start.

Chapter 14

Time Has No Age

Time has no age; I will repeat that statement, TIME has no AGE. It does not matter if you were 18 when you began your journey or you are 74. It's man who wants you to believe that if you haven't accomplished something by a certain age, you've missed the boat. Well, I'm here to tell you, that's a false belief, that's simply not true. Let's make a pact, you and I; from here on out, we are burying our old belief system of ourselves, those things that no longer serve our life. Instead, I challenge you to say to yourself, "That may have been my belief before, but not anymore." I'll be very transparent with you; the age factor played a major role in stopping me for going after my goals for a long time.

You gotta remember by the time I was 19 years of age, I was told by a record executive that I was too old for the industry and that they were only signing young singers between the ages of 11-16. Now, what you really must understand is that music was my entire world! So, to have an executive tell me that, I absolutely believed it to be true. It may have been true for that particular label and record executive but didn't mean it was true for the other labels. After all, prior to my car accident, two deals were on the table with Warner and Sony (surely another label would have come along), but instead of having my attorney shop my project around any further, those words stuck to my heart, and I played them in my sub conscious mind over and over again. For more than 18 years, I let fear of rejection consume me and stopped me from going after my dreams.

Another thing that helped me overcome my fear of failure was reading other peoples success stories. Being in the music industry, I researched entertainers who were over 30 that went from rags to riches. Now for you, it could be someone in your field of interest or just other people's stories in general that can inspire you. I was encouraged when I read stories like Taraji P. Henson - a single mother, who moved to Los Angeles with $700 in her pocket and her son. She spent two years struggling, eating peanut butter and jelly sandwiches, or the 99 cent dollar menu from McDonald- at the age of 27. She landed her first small-screen role, but it wasn't until she was 31 that she got a role opposite of Tyrese Gibson in the film Baby Boy. That was her breakout moment for a major film, and now she is a megastar on Empire and several other major films.

Or like Samuel L Jackson who at the age of 43 was heavily under the influence of alcohol, crack cocaine and heroin. In fact, it was Spike Lee who discovered him to play a crackhead in the film Jungle Fever. That role gave him the push to want to check into a rehab program and get his life together, free from drugs. But it wasn't until age 46 that led him to the role in Pulp Fiction, that made him a star and since then, Samuel Jackson has acted in 163 films. What a great story!

Stories like Sylvester Stallone who was a struggling actor and had a speech impairment, who at one point ended up homeless and slept at the New York bus station for 3 days. His lowest point was when he sold his dog for $25 because he didn't have any money to feed the dog anymore. One day, he saw a boxing match between the late great Mohammed Ali and Chuck Wepner, which inspired him to write the script of his famous movie Rocky! The studios loved the script, however, Sylvester wanted to star in the film as the main character and was rejected over and over again, they said he talked funny and looked funny. Despite that, several offers were made to purchase his script as much as $350k, but Mr. Stallone had a vision and would not bend. Finally, they agreed to let him star in it but only paid him $35K. That bet on himself, has made him the star he is today.

And I can't leave out another Icon of mine, Mr. Tyler Perry. Tyler's childhood was marked by sexual abuse and bitterness, at the age of 28 Tyler Perry wrote the stage play I Know I've Been Changed, but after several unsuccessful shows, he found himself living on the streets in Atlanta. Tyler was consistent, and eventually, this paid off for him and today his is a successful actor, playwright, and filmmaker. Forbes has him listed as the highest paid man in entertainment earning $130 million in 2010-2011. Now friends I personally know, have had the pleasure of being in several of his major films and plays, touring the world with him. Tyler Perry is a person I truly look up to and one-day hope to also have the pleasure of working with.

You may have noticed all of those entertainers mentioned above were actors, so my question was, were there any recording artist who released their first albums after age 30? I needed to have a reference from someone directly in my field of work, around the same age as me, to really give me hope that it was possible. As I began my quest, I discovered artists like Bill Withers, who at the age of 34 released his debut album "Just as I Am" in 1971, which featured his single "Ain't no Sunshine" it was that song that won him a Grammy. At 35, James Murphy recorded his self-titled debut album earning a Grammy Award nomination for Best Electronic/Dance Album.

Sheryl Crow was rejected by a label, so she began self-promoting her debut album that began gaining public attention. At the age of 31, she finally started seeing success. Let's not leave out another favorite of mine Pharrell Williams, he was already known as a producer, but the "Happy" singer didn't come out as an artist until he was 40.

Reading those types of stories gave me hope; they encouraged me and showed me that if they could do it despite their adversities, or age, then so could I. I had never written a play until I wrote a play. I had never released an album until I released an album and the chapters of your life will never be written if you don't take that step to write it.

You may not know, how your dreams will come true, where the funds will come from, or even who will support you. Look at me, I've never written a book until now. I was scared out of my mind, to put to paper my thoughts about my life and what I've learned along my journey.

It was fear of thinking no one would care and that no one wanted to hear my story etc., yet here we are, it's published, and you are literally reading it right now! Will it become a best seller and end up on Oprah's 'Must read'? Only time will tell. Just the fact, that I'm putting it out there, makes it possible it will get picked up. Someone may be reading my book that personally knows her and gives her a copy and just like that, Oprah is talking about my book and wants to meet me. Or someone who is an influencer writes a blog on my book, and it spreads like wildfire. Image me being a Best Seller or hitting Number 1 New Release! It's possible, but only because I stepped out on faith.

Hey, it can happen! Even if five people bought my book and those five people were my family and personal friends. The fact that I stepped out of my comfort zone and accomplished something that I've always wanted to do is an accomplishment. I am sitting here right now, patting myself on the back! Remember no one will believe in your dreams if you don't believe in them or yourself.

Which leads me to another word of advice, I have an 'Accomplishment Book' that I write in on a daily basis. Everything I've accomplished in my life, I write down big or small. Even if it's for example, "I accomplished waking up to see another day in my right state of mind". This will help you in your times of discouragement. Look at that book and you'll discover all of the wonderful things you have done. Take that one step, then take another, believe enough in you to know and understand that the world wants and needs whatever your talents and creations are.

We are waiting on you to discover the next X, build the next X, so go ahead, open that business, start that clothing line, study those lines and keep auditioning, go back to school gain some additional skills, whatever IT is, we are waiting.

Chapter 15

Practical Steps

So let's recap some practical steps you can do to overcome your fear of failure. Realize it's never too late to go after your dreams. Those visions in your head are God's indicators for you. He gives us all gifts and talents. Some people's gifts are to help others, like nurses and doctors. Some people's skills are to teach or build things. Some people's contributions are on the creative side, like photographers who capture beautiful images and some people's talents are musically inclined. Music is God's gift to me. Even when I would try to run away from it, I was always drawn back to it. Music is in my heartbeat, like a magnet that has a firm hold on me. Music is my escape – it is a way to express myself. It's healing, and it's love. Music is universal; it can motivate you or help you get through certain things. Whatever your talent or gift are, go for it.

Understand it doesn't matter when you start. Your race, age, gender, or your sexuality doesn't matter. So what! If you're now in your late 40's, so what! If you're recently divorced or in college, that does not mean it can't happen for you, none of that matters. All that matters is that you take that first step, and the next one, and the next one. Take me for instance, I've been going after my dreams since I was a teenager, and I've made no secret of me feeling like I'm nowhere near my goal. I let fear be my stumbling block. I thought I had missed the boat due to my age, my weight and I thought I wasn't pretty enough. There were so many fear factors. I thought the world wouldn't care about what I had to say.

The greatest fear that stopped me dead in my tracks were the thought, "What if I failed?" I recall waking up one day saying to myself,

"Why not me? I'm just as worthy, talented, and creative as the next person." I realized I was in my own way, besides, what did I have to lose? Write out your goals. All of those visions and images that come to you are blueprints. After you've written out your plan, you have to take action. A plan with no action will never work and will most certainly fail. Put one foot in front of the other and work daily towards your goals.

Think of babies: As they learn to walk, they start off inching their way along the floor. The scooting turns into a crawl and then the crawl turns into attempting to stand. As a baby tries to stand, their legs are wobbly; they even may have to use something to help them stand (i.e., your family for support). Eventually, they have the strength to pull themselves up and stand firmly. Once babies gain their balance, they slowly start to take one step and another then another. Those wobbly steps eventually lead to long strides and even running. They successfully master it and so can you.

Grasp the concept that there will be bumps along the way. There will be detours and distractions. I heard something recently by Joel Osteen, who mentioned that when building a home, an architect isn't worried about the appearance of how things look, how unorganized and messy it may seem. For he knows that when he starts each project, the home doesn't look like much but he has the blueprints written out in his mind and sees the end results. He anticipates the bumps along the road, i.e., rejections, disappointments, betrayal and so forth. However, with his blueprint or rather end goal firmly in his mind, he keeps going.

You see, that's the same thing with God: He has a plan for our lives. It may not be going the way you envision it. You may have to take some detours along the way; you may even discover while on this journey that He leads you down another path or that the people you start the journey with may not be there in the end. They may just be what I call "seasonal" helpers, that God sends your way". But God has a plan for your life, and He gives you these visions, He also gives you the free will. Will you trust Him to take that leap and know that He's got you? Or will you continue to be afraid and never go for anything? I'm hoping you choose to take that chance on yourself. You are worth it!

Last, face your fear of failure. You must understand failures are just lessons learned of what to do and what not to do. Failure is an opportunity to begin again and grow from it.

We all know the story of Thomas Edison; he made over a thousand attempts before he successfully invented the light bulb. You must continue forward in spite of your setbacks.

For you only truly fail when you stop trying.

You can succeed!

Afterword

May this book encourage you to face your fears and turn your dreams into reality; even your small steps, are a step in the right direction. Life will have ups and downs, but you are not alone. I could have written only about my good times, but that's not real reality. The real reality is that along the way, you are going to get some bumps and bruises, and crazy twist and turns. Pray about it, and I urge you to take flight, set sail, jump off that cliff and know that God has you. Don't live your life with what ifs.

It's true, I had a fear of failure, a fear of not living up to my boys' expectation of me, a fear that I would never amount to anything, a fear that I wasn't good enough and that my dreams and goals would never happen for me and I'll just stay stagnant. But, what helped me keep going is knowing that I can't live my life with regret or fear. Yes, it's natural to have a fear of failure, but I'm even more scared of not trying. Don't live with regret.

Personal Notes

What are your fears of failure?
_____
_____
_____
_____
_____

What are your dreams?
_____
_____
_____
_____
_____

What is your why? Your motivating factor (is it your family etc)?
_____
_____
_____
_____
_____

What is the first step you are going to take to overcome your fear?

_____
_____
_____
_____
_____
_____

What's your next step after that?

_____
_____
_____
_____
_____
_____

What are your take away(s) from this book

_____
_____
_____
_____
_____
_____

List 3 affirmations that you will say to yourself daily

_____
_____
_____
_____
_____

Quotes I Live By

"Too many of us are not living our dreams because we are living our fears." Les Brown

"God would not have put a dream in your heart if He had not already given you everything you need to fulfill it." Joel Osteen

"When you rule your mind, you rule your world. When you choose your thoughts, you choose results." Catherine Ponder

"All our dreams can come true if we have the courage to pursue them." Walt Disney

"Opportunities don't happen. You create them." Chris Grosser

"I have not failed. I've just found 10,000 ways that won't work." Thomas Edison

"There are two types of people who will tell you that you cannot make a difference in this world: those who are afraid to try and those who are afraid you will succeed." Ray Goforth

"The starting point of all achievement is desire." Napoleon Hill

"All progress takes place outside the comfort zone." Michael John Bobak

"Many of life's failures are people who did not realize how close they were to success when they gave up." Thomas A. Edison

"Would you like me to give you a formula for success? It's quite simple, really: Double your rate of failure. You are thinking of failure as the enemy of success. But it isn't at all. You can be discouraged by failure or you can learn from it, so go ahead and make mistakes. Make all you can. Because remember that's where you will find success." Thomas J. Watson

"There is a winner in you. You were created to be successful, to accomplish your goals, to leave your mark on this generation. You have greatness in you. The key is to get it out." Joel Osteen

"You are the only real obstacle in your path to a fulfilling life." Les Brown

"The biggest adventure you can ever take is to live the life of your dreams." Oprah Winfrey

Love Versus Fear
Poem by Mimosa Queen of life

As the morning sun rises and lights the earth
Birds sing a course of rebirth
A new day to begin
A new life to attend
Take a deep breath of fresh air
Exhale all of yesterday's fears held within
Open your eyes and mind
To thoughts and sites of new love
Love pure from the heart
As the rivers flow downstream
Leaving impurities among the rocks
Love easily knocks
Do you answer the door to your heart?
Or ignore it with fear blocking your start?
Knock once
Knock twice
Love begins to turn away
Fear stands in your way
How do I move this wall of shame?
I yell, "Move out the way!"
Fear stands saying, "NO WAY!" "
You're not going to make me miss my chance!" I say
Fear replies, "Oh Yes! And with a song and dance"
Love is walking slowly away.
Hearing this argument of fear standing in the way
Love sighs and says, "I'm going away"
I yell, "No Wait! Fear is in the way"

Love says, "Move him, so I can come to stay"
I push and pull
Yet fear won't budge
Love says, "I'm waiting for you to emerge"
Fear stands in the way
Grin on its face
Thinking it has won the race
Love knocks one more time with a force
That makes fear weak in the knees
I knew at that moment
I could be free
Pushing fear aside to let love come in
I open the door wide to my surprise
Fear fades away with feelings of defeat
　Love steps in filling my heart
With the warmth to succeed
See love conquers all
If we just believe

　Written by Mimosa Queen of Life Copyright@2015
QueenoflifeEmpowerment LLC

Call of Action

I'd love to hear your constructive opinion about my book. Receiving reviews from a wide variety of readers is excellent feedback for my growth. I appreciate your love and support on my new venture! Please share my links on your social media pages, write a review and share it on Amazon and purchase additional copies for your loved one(s). For bulk orders, contact me directly for discount!

Last, please shoot me a quick email or go to my site and subscribe to be added to my email list, for updates, free giveaways, and my upcoming tour dates.

I would love to speak at your next event, conference, school etc.

You can reach me at fearoffailurebook@gmail.com

Social Media Links
Facebook, Instagram, Twitter, LinkedIn
@FearofFailureBook

My musical links are listed under Butta B-Rocka
Buttabrocka.com

Social Media Links
Facebook, Instagram, Twitter, LinkedIn
@Buttabrocka Email: info@buttabrocka.com

My non-profit- Artists Rock the Mic Foundation
Artistsrockthemic.com

About the Author

International Touring Artist, Songwriter, Author of "Fear of Failure", Contributing Writer, Published Model, Actress, Playwright of the stage play "I Cheated So What", Humanitarian, CEO/Founder of 501c3 non-profit "Artists Rock the MIC Foundation" - Oleathia "Butta B-Rocka" Robinson has been diligently putting in work across markets and borders. Butta has redefined the term "versatility" by showcasing her vocals and composed pieces for ears in the US, UK, Germany, Holland, Japan, Canada, Portugal, St Lucia, St Thomas, St Kitts, Barbados, Chile, Puerto Rico, Antigua, Africa and across genres from pop, rock, gospel, country and rap.

Between her background vocals, demo recordings, and stage performances her résumé boasts work and assistance with international superstars, Grammy winners and performers like Janet Jackson, Akon, TLC, Nas, rock group Collective Soul, country singer Zac Brown, Dream, Japanese star Namie Amuro, Belgium superstar Sandrine,

German Artist Vanessa Jean Dedmon and countless other talents across the globe.

Butta started work on her own material and released her independently produced debut album, 'Switch Lanes.' This superstar uses her astonishing abilities as a musician and vocalist to render electrifying performances for corporate functions, conventions, private events as well as 5-star hotels. She has wooed domestic and international crowds in intimate settings as well as crowds that numbered well into the thousands. More specifically, The Coalition of Black Women Celebrating Legacy Anniversary performing for Rev. Dr. Bernice King (The King Center), Judge Penny Reynolds, Mr. Phil Wise (The Carter Center), Atlanta City Council President Felicia Moore, Ambassador Andrew Young, Former Atlanta Mayor Shirley Franklin, Dr. Joseph E. Lowery.

She has performed for: The CEO Network Bahamas Conference (Dr. Debbie Bartlett) for the Prime Minister of Bahamas, Her Royal Highness Princess Dr. Moradeun Ogunlana, & Princess Moradeun Adedoyin-Solarin and a host of other prestigious leaders. She has also performed at: BET Hip Hop Awards, The KY Derby, The Presidential Inauguration, The City Gala, International Cruise Lines as a guest entertainer for (The Seabourn, Royal Caribbean, Holland America, Norwegian), Duke University's Presidential Dance, Pink Affair Breast Cancer Fundraiser, Centennial Park, and various country clubs and casinos.

Butta continues to raise the bar! Named Hottest Female Vocalist 2017 & 2018 along with the 2018 CARE Award for her contributions to the community with her organization at the ATL'S Hottest Entertainment Awards and also nominated for Best Female R&B Artist of the year by the GA Music Awards, listed as 1 of the Top 4 Female R&B artist's in Georgia! She is currently in the studio working on her long-awaited sophomore album.

Butta is CEO/Founder of Artists Rock the M-I-C, bringing artists together from all genres of music and forms of art to impact a change working with the homeless college students. She believes in using her talents to heal and help others who don't have a voice. In 2016 Artists Rock the MIC Foundation 501c3 Non-Profit was created.

Dedicated to maintaining optimal professionalism, Butta holds membership with the Grammys, SESAC, BMI, Georgia Music, and NARIP. She currently attends Ashford University and will graduate with an all honors double major in Public Relations and Marketing. She serves as the 1st Black President for the Atlanta Chapter of the Golden Key International High Honor Society, and is a member of Alpha Sigma Lambda; she also has a BA degree in computer information systems.

Book Me

www.ingramcontent.com/pod-product-compliance
Lightning Source LLC
Chambersburg PA
CBHW071413290426
44108CB00014B/1806